Your Go-To Stir Cookbook

Easy, Effortless Stir Fry Cooking

BY: SOPHIA FREEMAN

© 2020 Sophia Freeman All Rights Reserved

✦ ✦ ✦ ✦ ✦ ✦ ✦ ★ ✦ ✦ ✦ ✦ ✦

COPYRIGHTED

Liability

This publication is meant as an informational tool. The individual purchaser accepts all liability if damages occur because of following the directions or guidelines set out in this publication. The Author bears no responsibility for reparations caused by the misuse or misinterpretation of the content.

Copyright

The content of this publication is solely for entertainment purposes and is meant to be purchased by one individual. Permission is not given to any individual who copies, sells or distributes parts or the whole of this publication unless it is explicitly given by the Author in writing.

★ ★ ★ ★ ★ ★ ★ ★ ★ ★ ★

Table of Contents

Introduction 7

    Steak Pepper Stir Fry 10

    Beef Broccoli Stir Fry 13

    Beef, Ginger Bok Choy 16

    Orange Beef Broccolini Stir Fry 19

    Steak with Cauliflower Rice 23

    Beef Spring Veggies 27

    Beef Veggies in Peanut Sauce 31

    Steak Noodles 34

    Beef Mango Stir Fry 37

    Beef Cabbage Stir Fry 41

    Chicken Peanut Stir Fry 44

    Cashew Chicken 48

    Chicken Veggies with Brown Rice 52

    Chicken Tofu Stir Fry 55

    Chicken Pad Thai 58

Chicken Pineapple Stir Fry 61

Sesame Honey Chicken 64

Chicken Broccoli Stir Fry 67

Teriyaki Chicken Stir Fry 70

Kung Pao Chicken 73

Pork Apple Stir Fry 76

Pork Green Bean Stir Fry 79

Pork Pineapple Fried Rice 82

Pork Kimchi Stir Fry 85

Pork with Zucchini Eggplant 88

Pork with Bok Choy Bell Pepper 92

Sweet Sour Pork 95

Pork Chop Suey 99

Pork with Napa Cabbage 102

Pork Spaghetti Squash Stir Fry 105

Vegetables Fried Rice 108

Snap Pea Asparagus Stir Fry 112

Carrot Pea Pod Stir Fry 115

Ginger Veggies Stir Fry 118

Vegetable Curry.. 121

Okra Stir Fry 124

Bok Choy Stir Fry... 127

Cabbage Carrots Stir Fry 130

Broccoli Tomato Stir Fry.. 133

Garden Stir Fry... 136

Tofu Mushroom Stir Fry 139

Szechuan Tofu... 142

Korean Tofu 145

Tofu with Cashews Peas... 150

Maple Barbecue Tofu... 153

Shrimp Fried Rice... 157

Shrimp in Hoisin Sauce 160

Salt Pepper Shrimp 163

Shrimp with Mango Spicy Basil... 166

Shrimp with Eggplant Green Beans.. 169

Conclusion.. 172

About the Author 173

Author's Afterthoughts 174

Introduction

Most people today don't have the luxury of time to make elaborate dishes in the kitchen.

It's primarily for this reason that stir fry dishes have amassed immense popularity worldwide, especially in countries with fast-paced societies.

A cooking method that originated in China thousands of years ago, stir frying involves frying meat and veggies in hot oil.

Some of the most common ingredients used for stir fry dishes include chicken, beef, shrimp, tofu, pork, turkey, onion, garlic, bell pepper, water chestnuts, carrots, broccoli, cauliflower, and pea pods. But of course, there are many other ingredients that you can use to make an appetizing and flavorful stir fry dish.

Although this cooking method is relatively easy, there are some techniques that you can follow to make sure you get it right.

Here are some worth considering:

- Prepare all the ingredients required in the recipe before you start cooking. Put them beside the stove so you can reach them easily and avoid burning the food.
- Slice vegetables and meat thinly for quicker cooking.
- Use a cast-iron pan if possible.
- Reduce heat when cooking aromatics.
- Use a sauce to thicken the stir fry.

In this book, you will find 50 amazing stir fry recipes that are not only enticing and flavorful but are also healthy and easy to prepare.

According to experts, stir frying is a healthy form of cooking method that helps retain the nutrients in vegetables.

Not only that, it's also a great way to add more vegetables to your dishes.

Even kids who are not that fond of eating veggies do not mind eating carrots, broccoli, or cauliflower when they are mixed with their favorite beef, chicken, pork, or shrimp.

Plus, some of these recipes can also be tweaked to suit the vegetarian diet. Simply omit the meat in the recipe and include only the vegetables, and that's it.

So are you ready to give these recipes a try?

Then it's time to take out your wok or frying pan.

Steak Pepper Stir Fry

Want something quick and easy for dinner? Stir fry steak strips with vegetables, and season with soy sauce and spices. This dish is ready in 30 minutes or less.

Serving Size: 6

Preparation Cooking Time: 30 minutes

Ingredients:

- ¼ cup reduced-sodium soy sauce
- 1 tablespoon chili-garlic sauce
- 1 teaspoon granulated sugar
- 2 teaspoons freshly grated ginger
- Salt to taste
- 1 tablespoon cornstarch
- 1 lb. steak, fat trimmed and sliced
- 2 tablespoons sesame oil, divided
- 1 cup onion, sliced
- 1 yellow bell pepper, sliced
- 1 cup sugar snap peas, sliced
- 2 cloves garlic, sliced thinly
- ¼ cup water
- 3 cups brown rice, cooked
- ½ cup scallions, sliced
- Fresh cilantro leaves, chopped

Instructions:

1. In a bowl, mix the soy sauce, chili garlic sauce, sugar, ginger, salt and cornstarch.

2. Transfer half of the mixture to another bowl. Set aside

3. Add the steak in the first bowl and coat evenly.

4. Pour 1 tablespoon sesame oil in a pan over medium high heat.

5. Cook the onion, bell pepper and snap peas for 2 minutes, stirring often.

6. Stir in the garlic.

7. Cook for 1 minute.

8. Transfer the vegetables to a plate.

9. Add the remaining oil into the pan.

10. Cook the beef for 2 minutes, stirring frequently.

11. Add the vegetables, reserved sauce and water.

12. Stir fry for 1 minute.

13. Place on top of cooked rice and sprinkle the scallions on top.

14. Garnish with the cilantro.

Nutrients per Serving:

- Calories 319
- Fat 10 g
- Saturated fat 2 g
- Carbohydrates 36 g
- Fiber 3 g
- Protein 21 g
- Cholesterol 11 mg
- Sugars 4 g
- Sodium 560 mg
- Potassium 350 mg

Beef Broccoli Stir Fry

This is even better than the beef and broccoli stir fry that you love to order in Chinese restaurants. This one includes more vegetables but tones down on fat and sodium. Not only that, it also only takes about 30 minutes to prepare.

Serving Size: 4

Preparation Cooking Time: 30 minutes

Ingredients:

- ¼ cup low-sodium soy sauce
- 2 tablespoons light brown sugar
- 2 tablespoons cornstarch, divided
- ¼ cup reduced-sodium chicken stock
- 1 lb. sirloin steak, sliced thinly
- 3 tablespoons vegetable oil, divided
- 6 cups broccoli florets
- 1 teaspoon garlic, grated
- 1 tablespoon ginger, grated
- ½ cup scallions, chopped
- 2 cups brown rice, cooked
- Red pepper flakes

Instructions:

1. Combine the soy sauce, brown sugar, half of cornstarch, and stock in a bowl.

2. Coat the steak strips with the remaining cornstarch.

3. Pour 2 tablespoons vegetable oil in a pan over medium heat.

4. Cook the steak strips for 4 minutes.

5. Transfer the steak to a plate.

6. Pour the remaining oil into the pan.

7. Cook the broccoli for 2 minutes, stirring often.

8. Add the garlic, ginger and scallions.

9. Stir fry for 30 seconds.

10. Add the soy sauce mixture to the pan.

11. Cook for 1 minute.

12. Serve with the brown rice and sprinkle the red pepper flakes on top.

Nutrients per Serving:

- Calories 440
- Fat 16 g
- Saturated fat 3.7 g
- Carbohydrates 43.2 g
- Fiber 4.5 g
- Protein 30 g
- Cholesterol 59 mg
- Sugars 9 g
- Sodium 741 mg
- Potassium 781 mg

Beef, Ginger Bok Choy

When you start to cook this at home, for sure, people are going to flock to the kitchen to see what's cooking. The aroma is simply irresistible. You'd love that this dish is also very easy to prepare.

Serving Size: 4

Preparation Cooking Time: 30 minutes

Ingredients:

- 1 ½ teaspoons low-sodium soy sauce
- 1 teaspoon dry sherry
- 1 tablespoon ginger, minced
- 1 tablespoon dry sherry
- 1 teaspoon cornstarch
- 12 oz. steak, fat trimmed and sliced into strips
- 1 teaspoon toasted sesame oil
- 2 tablespoons oyster sauce
- 1 tablespoon vegetable oil
- 8 cups bok choy
- 3 tablespoons chicken stock (unsalted)

Instructions:

1. In a bowl, mix the soy sauce, 1 teaspoon sherry, ginger and cornstarch.

2. Soak the beef in this mixture.

3. Stir in the sesame oil.

4. In another bowl, mix the oyster sauce and 1 tablespoon sherry. Set aside.

5. Pour the vegetable oil into a pan over medium high heat.

6. Cook the beef for 1 to 2 minutes.

7. Stir fry until brown.

8. Transfer to a plate.

9. Pour the stock into the pan.

10. Add the bok choy and cook for 2 minutes.

11. Put the beef back to the pan along with the reserved sauce.

12. Stir fry for 1 minute.

Nutrients per Serving:

- Calories 247
- Fat 12.8 g
- Saturated fat 4 g
- Carbohydrates 6.3 g
- Fiber 1.1 g
- Protein 25.5 g
- Cholesterol 69 mg
- Sugars 3 g
- Sodium 569 mg
- Potassium 765 mg

Orange Beef Broccolini Stir Fry

This is a delightful alternative to your favorite beef and broccoli stir fry. Instead of broccoli, we use broccolini. We also add oranges and red bell pepper to make the dish more colorful and delicious.

Serving Size: 4

Preparation Cooking Time: 40 minutes

Ingredients:

- ¼ cup freshly squeezed orange juice
- 1 tablespoon freshly grated orange zest
- 2 tablespoons unsweetened orange marmalade
- ¼ cup low-sodium beef stock
- 1 tablespoon chili garlic sauce
- 2 tablespoons low-sodium soy sauce
- 1 tablespoon cornstarch
- 1 teaspoons toasted sesame oil
- Cooking spray
- 12 oz. beef strips
- 2 teaspoons vegetable oil
- 1 tablespoon freshly grated ginger
- 6 cloves garlic, crushed and minced
- 8 oz. broccolini, sliced into small pieces
- 6 scallions, sliced
- 1 red bell pepper, sliced into strips
- 2 oranges, sliced into sections
- 1 tablespoon sesame seeds
- 4 cups cooked brown rice

Instructions:

1. Mix the orange juice, orange zest, orange marmalade, beef stock, chili garlic sauce, soy sauce, cornstarch and sesame oil in a bowl. Set aside.

2. Spray your pan with oil.

3. Place the pan over medium heat.

4. Stir fry the beef for 3 minutes.

5. Transfer to a plate.

6. Pour the vegetable oil into the pan.

7. Cook the ginger and garlic for 30 seconds.

8. Stir in the broccolini. Cook for 3 minutes.

9. Add the scallions and bell pepper. Stir fry for 2 to 3 minutes.

10. Put the beef back to the skillet along with the reserved sauce.

11. Cook for 1 minute or until thick.

12. Add the oranges.

13. Cook for 1 minute.

14. Add the beef and vegetables on top of the brown rice.

15. Sprinkle the sesame seeds on top.

Nutrients per Serving:

- Calories 355
- Fat 10.9 g
- Saturated fat 2.5 g
- Carbohydrates 41.5 g
- Fiber 5.3 g
- Protein 23.2 g
- Cholesterol 48 mg
- Sugars 13 g
- Sodium 470 mg
- Potassium 772 mg

Steak with Cauliflower Rice

Do you want to tone down your carb intake? Replace rice with cauliflower rice when you make this beef stir fry dish.

Serving Size: 4

Preparation Cooking Time: 30 minutes

Ingredients:

- 8 oz. sirloin steak, sliced thinly
- 1 tablespoon dry sherry
- 4 tablespoons low-sodium soy sauce, divided
- 4 tablespoons vegetable oil, divided
- 2 eggs, beaten
- 4 scallions, sliced
- 1 cup carrots, diced
- 2 cloves garlic, crushed and minced
- 1 tablespoon ginger, minced
- 1 cup frozen peas
- 4 cups cauliflower rice
- 1 teaspoon sesame oil
- 2 teaspoons sesame seeds, toasted

Instructions:

1. Coat the steak with the dry sherry and 1 tablespoon soy sauce.

2. Pour 1 teaspoon vegetable oil into a pan over medium heat.

3. Cook the eggs while stirring for 1 minute.

4. Transfer the egg to a bowl.

5. Increase heat.

6. Pour 2 teaspoons vegetable oil into the pan.

7. Add the steak.

8. Stir fry for 3 minutes.

9. Transfer to a plate.

10. Pour 2 tablespoons vegetable oil into the pan.

11. Cook the scallions and carrots for 4 minutes, stirring often.

12. Add the garlic, ginger and peas.

13. Stir fry for 3 minutes.

14. Transfer to the plate with the steak.

15. Pour the remaining oil into the pan.

16. Cook the cauliflower rice for 5 minutes, stirring often.

17. Stir in the beef, eggs and vegetables.

18. Season with the remaining soy sauce.

19. Drizzle the sesame oil and sprinkle the sesame seeds on top.

Nutrients per Serving:

- Calories 355
- Fat 21.6 g
- Saturated fat 3.3 g
- Carbohydrates 15.2 g
- Fiber 5 g
- Protein 22.1 g
- Cholesterol 128 mg
- Sugars 6 g
- Sodium 853 mg
- Potassium 443 mg

Beef Spring Veggies

There's no more need to dine in a restaurant just to get a taste of your favorite beef stir fry. This dish, which includes thin strips of beef sirloin and spring vegetables, packs in more flavor and nutrients. Drizzle with citrus sauce and serve with brown rice.

Serving Size: 6

Preparation Cooking Time: 40 minutes

Ingredients:

- ¼ cup freshly squeezed orange juice
- 2 tablespoons low-sodium soy sauce
- 2 tablespoons rice vinegar
- 3 tablespoons mirin
- 2 teaspoons cornstarch
- 2 tablespoons miso paste
- 2 tablespoons vegetable oil
- 1 ½ lb. beef sirloin steak, sliced thinly
- 1 cup carrots, sliced
- 2 cups snow peas
- 6 cloves garlic, crushed and minced
- 4 teaspoons ginger, minced
- 1 cup red sweet pepper, sliced into strips
- 6 stalks green onion, sliced
- 3 cups wild mushrooms, chopped
- 1 teaspoon sesame seeds, toasted
- 2 cups brown rice, cooked

Instructions:

1. In a bowl, mix the orange juice, soy sauce, rice vinegar, mirin, cornstarch and miso paste.

2. In a pan over medium high heat, add 1 tablespoon vegetable oil.

3. Cook the beef for 3 minutes, stirring often.

4. Transfer to a plate.

5. Add the remaining oil to the pan.

6. Cook the carrots and snow peas.

7. Stir fry for 3 minutes.

8. Add the garlic, ginger and sweet pepper.

9. Stir fry for 1 minute.

10. Stir in the green onions and mushrooms.

11. Cook for 3 minutes.

12. Transfer to a plate.

13. Add the sauce to the pan.

14. Cook until the sauce has thickened.

15. Put the beef and veggies back to the pan.

16. Coat with the sauce.

17. Simmer for 1 minute.

18. Sprinkle the sesame seeds on top and serve with the brown rice.

Nutrients per Serving:

- Calories 350
- Fat 10.4 g
- Saturated fat 2.2 g
- Carbohydrates 32.8 g
- Fiber 3.9 g
- Protein 30.7 g
- Cholesterol 68 mg
- Sugars 10 g
- Sodium 557 mg
- Potassium 818 mg

Beef Veggies in Peanut Sauce

This dish is loaded with Asian flavors that you just can't get enough of. This is also an ideal option if you're running late but don't want to rely on instant food or takeout for your family's dinner.

Serving Size: 2

Preparation Cooking Time: 20 minutes

Ingredients:

- 3 tablespoons peanut butter powder
- ½ cup cold water
- 1 tablespoon cider vinegar
- 1 tablespoon low-sodium teriyaki sauce
- ¼ teaspoon red pepper flakes
- ¼ teaspoon ground ginger
- 2 teaspoons honey
- Cooking spray
- 1 clove garlic, crushed and minced
- 6 oz. beef sirloin, sliced into strips
- ½ cup carrots, shredded
- 1 cup snow peas, trimmed
- 2 cups brown rice, cooked

Instructions:

1. Add the peanut butter sauce to a bowl with the cold water.

2. Stir until the powder has dissolved.

3. Stir in the vinegar, teriyaki sauce, red pepper flakes, ginger and honey.

4. Transfer to a pan over medium heat.

5. Bring to a boil.

6. Reduce heat and simmer for 2 minutes or until the sauce has thickened.

7. Spray your pan with oil.

8. Stir fry the garlic and beef for 2 minutes.

9. Add the carrots and peas.

10. Cook while stirring for 2 minutes.

11. Stir in the peanut sauce.

12. Stir to coat the beef and vegetables evenly.

13. Cook for 2 minutes, stirring often.

14. Serve with the cooked brown rice.

Nutrients per Serving:

- Calories 353
- Fat 12 g
- Saturated fat 4 g
- Carbohydrates 36 g
- Fiber 3 g
- Protein 26 g
- Cholesterol 34 mg
- Sugars 10 g
- Sodium 345 mg
- Potassium 556 mg

Steak Noodles

Infused with Asian flavors, this beef and noodles dish is sure to be a hit when you prepare it for your family. If you can't find soba noodles, you can also use spaghetti or rice noodles.

Serving Size: 4

Preparation Cooking Time: 50 minutes

Ingredients:

- 1 tablespoon garlic, crushed and minced
- 1 tablespoon ginger, minced
- 2 tablespoons freshly squeezed lime juice
- 3 tablespoons low-sodium soy sauce, divided
- 1 tablespoon brown sugar
- 1 lb. flank steak, fat trimmed and sliced into thin strips
- Water
- 8 oz. buckwheat soba noodles
- 12 oz. broccoli slaw
- 1 tablespoon sesame seeds, toasted
- 1 tablespoon toasted sesame oil
- 1 tablespoon peanut oil

Instructions:

1. Add the garlic, ginger, lime juice, 2 tablespoons soy sauce, and brown sugar in a bowl.

2. Stir in the steak and coat evenly with the sauce.

3. Cover the bowl with foil.

4. Chill in the refrigerator for 30 minutes.

5. Fill a pot with water.

6. Bring to a boil.

7. Add the noodles and prepare according to the directions in the package.

8. Add the broccoli slaw in the last 1 minute of cooking the noodles.

9. Drain and rinse under cool running water.

10. Transfer the noodles and slaw in a bowl.

11. Toss the noodles in the remaining soy sauce, sesame seeds and sesame oil.

12. Add the peanut oil into a pan over medium heat.

13. Stir fry the steak for 5 minutes.

14. Serve the steak on top of the noodles.

Nutrients per Serving:

- Calories 495
- Fat 15.9 g
- Saturated fat 3.8 g
- Carbohydrates 54.5 g
- Fiber 5.5 g
- Protein 34.6 g
- Cholesterol 69 mg
- Sugars 6 g
- Sodium 486 mg
- Potassium 862 mg

Beef Mango Stir Fry

Stir fry beef, mango, basil, and bell peppers in fish sauce for a quick and simple but flavorful dinner meal. It's best to use cooked rice for this dish.

Serving Size: 4

Preparation Cooking Time: 35 minutes

Ingredients:

- 1 teaspoon peanut oil
- 2 eggs, beaten
- 2 tablespoons vegetable oil, divided
- 2 teaspoons garlic, minced
- 3 scallions, chopped
- 2 teaspoons ginger, grated
- 1 lb. strip steak, fat trimmed and sliced into strips
- 1 cup red bell pepper, diced
- 1 cup green bell pepper, diced
- 2 cups brown rice (cooked and refrigerated overnight)
- 2 tablespoons fish sauce
- 3 tablespoons freshly squeezed lime juice
- ½ cup mango, diced
- 2 tablespoons fresh basil leaves, chopped

Instructions:

1. Add the peanut oil to a pan over medium high heat.

2. Cook the eggs for 30 seconds.

3. Flip and cook for 15 seconds.

4. Transfer the eggs to a cutting board.

5. Slice into strips.

6. Add half of the vegetable oil to the pan.

7. Stir fry the garlic, scallions and ginger for 30 seconds.

8. Stir in the steak.

9. Cook for 1 minute.

10. Add the bell peppers.

11. Stir fry for 3 minutes.

12. Transfer the beef and veggies to a plate.

13. Pour the remaining oil into the pan.

14. Cook the rice while stirring for 2 minutes.

15. Put the beef and veggies back to the pan along with the eggs.

16. Stir in the fish sauce, lime juice, mango and basil.

17. Cook for 2 minutes.

Nutrients per Serving:

- Calories 417
- Fat 16.7 g
- Saturated fat 4.3 g
- Carbohydrates 35.7 g
- Fiber 4.5 g
- Protein 30.3 g
- Cholesterol 154 mg
- Sugars 6 g
- Sodium 694 mg
- Potassium 613 mg

Beef Cabbage Stir Fry

Delight your family and friends with this beef and cabbage stir fry flavored with spicy peanut sauce.

Serving Size: 4

Preparation Cooking Time: 40 minutes

Ingredients:

- ¼ cup peanut butter
- 3 tablespoons low-sodium soy sauce
- 1 tablespoon rice vinegar
- ⅓ cup freshly squeezed orange juice
- 2 teaspoons sugar
- 4 teaspoons vegetable oil, divided
- 3 cloves garlic, crushed and minced
- 1 lb. sirloin steak, fat trimmed and sliced thinly
- 1 head cabbage, sliced thinly
- 3 tablespoons water
- 2 carrots, grated
- ¼ cup roasted peanuts, chopped

Instructions:

1. In a bowl, combine the peanut butter, soy sauce, rice vinegar, orange juice and sugar.

2. Pour half of the vegetable oil into a pan over medium heat.

3. Cook the garlic for 30 seconds.

4. Add the steak and stir fry for 3 minutes.

5. Transfer to a plate.

6. Add the remaining oil to the pan.

7. Add the cabbage and water.

8. Cook for 4 minutes.

9. Add the carrots.

10. Cook for 3 minutes.

11. Put the beef back to the pan.

12. Add the peanut sauce and stir.

13. Sprinkle the peanuts on top and serve.

Nutrients per Serving:

- Calories 367
- Fat 17.4 g
- Saturated fat 3.3 g
- Carbohydrates 22.6 g
- Fiber 7.5 g
- Protein 30.3 g
- Cholesterol 59 mg
- Sugars 10 g
- Sodium 569 mg
- Potassium 854 mg

Chicken Peanut Stir Fry

Save time and energy preparing this dish by using pre-mixed broccoli slaw. Combine this with chicken strips and drizzle with peanut sauce, and you have a restaurant-worthy dinner meal.

Serving Size: 4

Preparation Cooking Time: 30 minutes

Ingredients:

- Water
- 4 oz. rice noodles
- 1 tablespoon fish sauce
- 2 tablespoons peanut butter
- 3 tablespoons freshly squeezed lime juice
- ½ teaspoon freshly grated lime zest
- 4 cloves garlic, crushed and minced
- 2 teaspoons chili bean sauce
- 1 tablespoon water
- 3 teaspoons vegetable oil
- 1 lb. chicken breast, sliced into strips
- 1 red sweet pepper, sliced into strips
- 3 green onions, sliced thinly
- 2 cups broccoli slaw mix
- 2 tablespoons peanuts, chopped

Instructions:

1. Fill a small pot with water.

2. Bring to a boil.

3. Remove from heat.

4. Add the noodles.

5. Let sit for 8 minutes.

6. Drain the water.

7. In a bowl, mix the fish sauce, peanut butter, lime juice, lime zest, garlic, chili bean sauce and 1 tablespoon water.

8. Mix well and set aside.

9. In a pan over medium high heat, cook the chicken for 5 minutes, stirring occasionally.

10. Transfer to a plate.

11. Add the remaining oil to the pan.

12. Cook the sweet pepper for 2 minutes.

13. Stir in the noodles and green onions.

14. Cook for 2 minutes.

15. Add the chicken, sauce and broccoli.

16. Cook while stirring for 1 minute.

17. Transfer to serving plates.

18. Garnish with the peanuts and serve.

Nutrients per Serving:

- Calories 368
- Fat 11.5 g
- Saturated fat 1.8 g
- Carbohydrates 33.7 g
- Fiber 3 g
- Protein 32.2 g
- Cholesterol 66 mg
- Sugars 4 g
- Sodium 556 mg
- Potassium 482 mg

Cashew Chicken

This dish is not only full of color but also packed with flavor and crunchy texture that you'd surely love.

Serving Size: 4

Preparation Cooking Time: 1 hour

Ingredients:

- 2 tablespoons low-sodium soy sauce
- 2 teaspoons toasted sesame oil
- 2 teaspoons freshly grated ginger
- 1 tablespoon cornstarch
- 12 oz. chicken breast fillet, sliced into strips
- 2 tablespoons oyster sauce
- 2 tablespoons water
- ¼ cup cashews, chopped
- 3 teaspoons vegetable oil, divided
- 1 onion, sliced into wedges
- 3 cloves garlic, crushed and minced
- 1 red sweet pepper, sliced
- 6 oz. snow pea pods, rinsed and drained
- 8 oz. water chestnuts, sliced

Instructions:

1. In a bowl, mix the soy sauce, sesame oil, ginger and cornstarch.

2. Add the chicken to the bowl.

3. Coat with the sauce evenly.

4. Cover the bowl with foil.

5. Marinate for 20 minutes.

6. In another bowl, mix the oyster sauce and water.

7. Add the cashews to a pan over medium high heat.

8. Toast for 3 minutes, stirring often.

9. Transfer to a plate.

10. Add 1 teaspoon vegetable oil to the pan.

11. Stir fry onion for 1 minute.

12. Add the garlic, sweet pepper and pea pods.

13. Cook while stirring for another 1 minute.

14. Add the water chestnuts.

15. Transfer the vegetables to a plate.

16. Pour the remaining oil to the pan.

17. Cook the chicken for 3 minutes.

18. Put the veggies back to the pan along with the reserved sauce.

19. Heat through.

20. Sprinkle the cashews on top and serve.

Nutrients per Serving:

- Calories 299
- Fat 12.5 g
- Saturated fat 1.9 g
- Carbohydrates 23 g
- Fiber 5.6 g
- Protein 24.6 g
- Cholesterol 49 mg
- Sugars 5 g
- Sodium 551 mg
- Potassium 483 mg

Chicken Veggies with Brown Rice

For a quick meal that's complete with essential nutrients, give this chicken and vegetable stir fry a try. It's best served with brown rice.

Serving Size: 5

Preparation Cooking Time: 30 minutes

Ingredients:

- 2 tablespoons dried mushrooms
- Hot water
- 2 teaspoons olive oil
- ½ cup onion, chopped
- ½ cup red sweet pepper, sliced
- ½ cup celery, sliced
- 15 oz. low-sodium chicken stock
- 3 cups cooked brown rice
- 4 carrots, sliced into thin sticks
- 10 oz. chicken breast, cooked and chopped
- 14 oz. canned artichoke hearts, drained and sliced into half
- 1 teaspoon poultry seasoning
- ½ teaspoon garlic and herb seasoning blend (unsalted)
- ¼ teaspoon garlic powder
- Salt and pepper to taste

Instructions:

1. Cover the mushrooms with hot water.

2. Let sit for 5 minutes.

3. Drain and chop the mushrooms. Set aside.

4. In a pan over medium heat, cook the onion, sweet pepper and celery for 5 minutes, stirring often.

5. Pour in the broth.

6. Add the mushrooms.

7. Bring to a boil.

8. Add the carrots.

9. Reduce heat and simmer for 5 minutes.

10. Stir in the chicken, cooked rice and the rest of the ingredients.

11. Cook while stirring for 2 to 3 minutes.

Nutrients per Serving:

- Calories 290
- Fat 4.9 g
- Saturated fat 0.9 g
- Carbohydrates 39.1 g
- Fiber 6.1 g
- Protein 23.1 g
- Cholesterol 48 mg
- Sugars 5 g
- Sodium 661 mg
- Potassium 428 mg

Chicken Tofu Stir Fry

Stir fry chicken, tofu, and vegetables for a light, delicious, and special dinner meal that you and your family will love.

Serving Size: 6

Preparation Cooking Time: 1 hour and 30 minutes

Ingredients:

- 2 tablespoons freshly squeezed orange juice
- 1 teaspoon dry mustard
- 2 tablespoons olive oil, divided
- 1 tablespoon Worcestershire sauce
- 1 tablespoon low-sodium soy sauce
- 1 teaspoon ground turmeric
- 8 oz. chicken breast, cooked and sliced into cubes
- 8 oz. tofu, sliced into cubes
- 2 carrots, sliced thinly
- 1 cup mushrooms
- 2 cups bean sprouts
- 1 red sweet pepper, sliced into strips
- 3 stalks green onion
- 3 cups brown rice, cooked

Instructions:

1. In a bowl, combine the orange juice, mustard, half of olive oil, Worcestershire sauce, soy sauce and turmeric.

2. Add the chicken and tofu.

3. Coat evenly.

4. Cover with foil.

5. Marinate in the refrigerator for 1 hour.

6. In a pan over medium heat, pour the remaining oil.

7. Stir fry the carrot for 2 minutes.

8. Add the mushrooms and cook for 2 minutes.

9. Stir in the bean sprouts, sweet pepper and green onions.

10. Stir fry for 2 minutes.

11. Add the chicken and cook for 3 to 5 minutes, stirring often.

12. Serve with the cooked brown rice.

Nutrients per Serving:

- Calories 285
- Fat 9.3 g
- Saturated fat 1.5 g
- Carbohydrates 30 g
- Fiber 3.9 g
- Protein 20.3 g
- Cholesterol 32 mg
- Sugars 4 g
- Sodium 331 mg
- Potassium 559 mg

Chicken Pad Thai

Here's a Chicken Pad Thai recipe that perfectly combines sweet, savory, and sour flavors. Like most stir-fry dishes, this one also takes only a few minutes to prepare.

Serving Size: 4

Preparation Cooking Time: 30 minutes

Ingredients:

- Water
- 6 oz. rice noodles
- 4 cups mung bean sprouts
- 12 oz. chicken thigh, sliced into smaller pieces
- 3 cloves garlic, crushed and minced
- 2 eggs, beaten
- 2 tablespoons peanut oil, divided
- 2 tablespoons fish sauce
- ¼ cup scallions, chopped
- ¼ cup rice vinegar
- ½ teaspoon red pepper flakes
- 2 tablespoons brown sugar
- ¼ cup roasted peanuts, chopped
- Lime wedges

Instructions:

1. Fill your pot with water.

2. Bring to a boil.

3. Add the noodles.

4. Cook for 6 to 7 minutes.

5. Drain the water.

6. Rinse the noodles under cool running water.

7. Pour 1 tablespoon peanut oil into a pan over medium high heat.

8. Add the chicken and stir fry for 5 minutes.

9. Transfer to a plate.

10. Add the remaining oil and stir fry the garlic for 15 seconds.

11. Add the eggs. Cook for 30 seconds.

12. Stir in the noodles, chicken and the rest of the ingredients except the peanuts and lime wedges.

13. Cook while stirring for 2 minutes.

14. Garnish with the peanuts and lime wedges before serving.

Nutrients per Serving:

- Calories 457
- Fat 17.4 g
- Saturated fat 3.6 g
- Carbohydrates 51.3 g
- Fiber 2.6 g
- Protein 24.7 g
- Cholesterol 173 mg
- Sugars 10 g
- Sodium 836 mg
- Potassium 487 mg

Chicken Pineapple Stir Fry

Get a taste of the tropics when you prepare this chicken and pineapple stir fry dish. It's ready in 20 minutes or less.

Serving Size: 4

Preparation Cooking Time: 20 minutes

Ingredients:

- 4 teaspoons vegetable oil, divided
- 1 onion, sliced in half
- 1 cup zucchini, sliced into strips
- ¾ cup pea pods, trimmed
- 1 cup pineapple chunks
- 3 chicken breast fillets, sliced into strips
- 3 tablespoons stir-fry sauce

Instructions:

1. Pour half of the vegetable oil into a pan over medium heat.

2. Stir fry the onion for 2 minutes.

3. Add the zucchini, pea pods and pineapple chunks.

4. Stir fry for 2 minutes.

5. Transfer to a plate.

6. Pour the remaining oil to the pan.

7. Cook the chicken for 3 minutes, stirring often.

8. Put the onion mixture back to the pan.

9. Pour in the stir fry sauce.

10. Cook for 1 minute.

11. Serve with the pineapple wedges.

Nutrients per Serving:

- Calories 203
- Fat 7 g
- Saturated fat 0.8 g
- Carbohydrates 13.9 g
- Fiber 1.6 g
- Protein 20.8 g
- Cholesterol 62 mg
- Sugars 9 g
- Sodium 430 mg
- Potassium 412 mg

Sesame Honey Chicken

Chicken and green beans sautéed in sesame honey sauce and served with rice—it's your go-to meal when you want something quick and delicious.

Serving Size: 2

Preparation Cooking Time: 40 minutes

Ingredients:

- 1 tablespoon low-sodium soy sauce
- 1 tablespoon honey
- 3 cloves garlic, crushed and minced
- 2 teaspoons freshly grated ginger
- Red pepper flakes
- Cooking spray
- 8 oz. chicken thigh, sliced into small pieces
- 1 teaspoon sesame oil
- 1 teaspoon vegetable oil
- 4 oz. green beans, trimmed and sliced
- 2 tablespoons shallots, chopped
- ⅔ cup cooked brown rice
- Toasted sesame seeds

Instructions:

1. Mix the soy sauce, honey, garlic, ginger and red pepper flakes in a bowl. Set aside.

2. Spray your pan with oil.

3. Cook the chicken for 10 minutes, stirring often.

4. Transfer the chicken to a plate.

5. Pour the sesame oil and vegetable oil into a pan over medium heat.

6. Stir fry the green beans for 2 minutes.

7. Add the shallots and stir fry for 1 minute.

8. Put the chicken back to the pan.

9. Pour the sauce into the pan.

10. Cook for 2 to 3 minutes or until the sauce has thickened.

11. Place the chicken mixture on top of the brown rice.

12. Sprinkle the toasted sesame seeds on top.

Nutrients per Serving:

- Calories 333
- Fat 10 g
- Saturated fat 2 g
- Carbohydrates 35 g
- Fiber 3 g
- Protein 26 g
- Cholesterol 108 mg
- Sugars 12 g
- Sodium 365 mg
- Potassium 442 mg

Chicken Broccoli Stir Fry

Here's a lighter version of your favorite of beef and broccoli stir fry. The addition of mango chutney can make this food even more special.

Serving Size: 4

Preparation Cooking Time: 30 minutes

Ingredients:

- 5 cups water
- 8 oz. whole-wheat capellini pasta
- 1 tablespoon sesame oil
- 2 teaspoons white vinegar
- 3 tablespoons low-sodium soy sauce
- ¼ cup reduced-sodium chicken stock
- 2 cloves garlic, grated
- 2 teaspoons cornstarch
- ¼ cup mango chutney
- ¼ teaspoon red pepper flakes
- 2 tablespoons grapeseed oil, divided
- 1 lb. chicken breast fillet
- 5 cups broccoli florets
- 1 cup scallions, chopped and divided

Instructions:

1. Fill a pot with water.

2. Add the pasta and cook for 3 minutes, stirring often.

3. Drain the water.

4. Toss the pasta in sesame oil.

5. In a bowl, mix the vinegar, soy sauce, chicken stock, garlic, cornstarch, mango chutney and red pepper flakes. Set aside.

6. Pour 1 tablespoon grapeseed oil into a pan over medium high heat.

7. Stir fry the chicken for 5 minutes.

8. Transfer to a plate.

9. Reduce heat and pour in the remaining oil.

10. Stir fry the scallions and broccoli for 3 minutes.

11. Put the chicken back to the pan.

12. Pour in the reserved sauce.

13. Cook for 2 minutes or until the sauce has thickened.

14. Serve with the pasta.

Nutrients per Serving:

- Calories 515
- Fat 14.8 g
- Saturated fat 2 g
- Carbohydrates 62.3 g
- Fiber 7.8 g
- Protein 33.9 g
- Cholesterol 63 mg
- Sugars 13 g
- Sodium 747 mg
- Potassium 800 mg

Teriyaki Chicken Stir Fry

Here's the version of teriyaki chicken that's lower in sugar and sodium. You can also use other veggies like green beans or carrots if you don't have broccoli.

Serving Size: 4

Preparation Cooking Time: 15 minutes

Ingredients:

- 1 tablespoon grapeseed oil
- 1 lb. chicken breast fillet, sliced into cubes
- 8 oz. broccoli florets
- 2 tablespoons pineapple juice
- ¼ cup reduced-sodium tamari
- 1 tablespoon rice vinegar
- 1 ½ tablespoons honey
- 1 teaspoon freshly grated ginger
- 2 teaspoons freshly grated garlic
- 2 teaspoons cornstarch
- 4 cups cooked brown rice
- 1 teaspoon toasted sesame seeds
- ¼ cup scallions, chopped

Instructions:

1. Pour the oil into a pan over medium high heat.

2. Stir fry the chicken for 6 minutes.

3. Add the broccoli and cook for 5 minutes.

4. In a bowl, mix the pineapple juice, tamari, vinegar, honey, ginger, garlic and cornstarch.

5. Add this to the pan.

6. Cook while stirring for 30 seconds.

7. Remove from the stove.

8. Serve the chicken and vegetables with the rice, garnished with the sesame seeds and scallions.

Nutrients per Serving:

- Calories 426
- Fat 8 g
- Saturated fat 1 g
- Carbohydrates 53 g
- Fiber 4 g
- Protein 35 g
- Cholesterol 76 mg
- Sugars 9 g
- Sodium 774 mg
- Potassium 733 mg

Kung Pao Chicken

You'd be surprised at how quickly you can prepare this amazing dish. The marinade not only infuses the chicken with incredible flavors but also tenderizes the meat.

Serving Size: 4

Preparation Cooking Time: 30 minutes

Ingredients:

- 1 lb. chicken breast fillet, sliced into strips
- 1 teaspoon dry sherry
- 2 teaspoons low-sodium soy sauce
- 2 teaspoons cornstarch
- 2 teaspoons sesame oil
- 1 tablespoon soy sauce
- 1 tablespoon dry sherry
- 2 teaspoons chili-garlic sauce
- 2 teaspoons balsamic vinegar
- 2 tablespoons reduced sodium chicken stock
- 2 tablespoons vegetable oil, divided
- 3 slices ginger, chopped
- 1 red bell pepper, diced
- 1 green bell pepper, diced
- Salt to taste
- 2 tablespoons roasted peanuts

Instructions:

1. Season the chicken strips with 1 teaspoon dry sherry and 2 teaspoons soy sauce.

2. Coat with the cornstarch and sesame oil.

3. In another bowl, mix 1 tablespoon sherry, 1 tablespoon soy sauce, chili garlic sauce, balsamic vinegar and chicken stock. Set aside.

4. Pour 1 tablespoon vegetable oil into a pan over medium heat.

5. Add the ginger and stir fry for 10 seconds.

6. Add the chicken and stir fry for 3 minutes.

7. Transfer to a plate.

8. Pour the remaining oil to the pan.

9. Stir fry the bell peppers for 1 minute.

10. Put the chicken back to pan along with the sauce.

11. Season with the salt.

12. Cook for 3 minutes.

13. Top with the peanuts and serve.

Nutrients per Serving:

- Calories 264
- Fat 14.4 g
- Saturated fat 2.5 g
- Carbohydrates 7.4 g
- Fiber 1.6 g
- Protein 25.2 g
- Cholesterol 63 mg
- Sugars 3 g
- Sodium 459 mg
- Potassium 477 mg

Pork Apple Stir Fry

The combination of apple jelly and apple juice creates a unique sauce for this pork stir fry.

Serving Size: 2

Preparation Cooking Time: 30 minutes

Ingredients:

- 1 ½ tablespoons apple jelly
- 2 tablespoons apple juice (unsweetened)
- 2 teaspoons low-sodium teriyaki sauce
- 2 teaspoons low-sodium soy sauce
- Red pepper flakes
- Cooking spray
- ¼ cup onion, sliced
- ¼ cup celery, chopped
- ½ cup red sweet pepper, sliced into strips
- 1 clove garlic, crushed and minced
- 1 teaspoon ginger, grated
- 2 tablespoons carrot, shredded
- ¼ cup apple strips
- 2 tablespoons water chestnuts, sliced
- 2 teaspoons sesame oil
- 6 oz. pork chops (boneless), sliced into strips
- 2 cups brown rice, cooked

Instructions:

1. In a bowl, mix the apple jelly, apple juice, teriyaki sauce, soy sauce and red pepper flakes. Set aside.

2. Spray your pan with oil.

3. Put it over medium high heat.

4. Stir fry the onion, celery and sweet pepper for 3 minutes.

5. Stir in the garlic, ginger, carrot, apple and water chestnuts.

6. Cook for 3 minutes.

7. Transfer to a plate.

8. Pour the sesame oil to the pan.

9. Stir fry the pork strips for 3 minutes.

10. Put the veggies back to the pan.

11. Add the sauce mixture.

12. Cook while stirring for 2 minutes.

13. Serve with the cooked rice.

Nutrients per Serving:

- Calories 294
- Fat 7.2 g
- Saturated fat 1.5 g
- Carbohydrates 38.6 g
- Fiber 3.6 g
- Protein 19.6 g
- Cholesterol 35 mg
- Sugars 16 g
- Sodium 498 mg
- Potassium 627 mg

Pork Green Bean Stir Fry

This savory dish made with pork and green beans drenched in Sichuan sauce.

Serving Size: 4

Preparation Cooking Time: 20 minutes

Ingredients:

- 2 tablespoons garlic, crushed and minced
- 5 small dried red chili
- 2 tablespoons peanut oil
- 2 tablespoons ginger, minced
- 1 lb. lean ground pork
- 1 ½ tablespoons dry sherry
- ½ teaspoon sugar
- 1 lb. green beans, trimmed and sliced in half
- ½ teaspoon cornstarch
- 3 tablespoons low-sodium tamari
- ½ teaspoon Chinese five-spice powder

Instructions:

1. In a pan over medium heat, cook the garlic, ginger and pork for 7 minutes.

2. Transfer to a plate.

3. In a bowl, mix the tamari, dry sherry, sugar, cornstarch and five-spice powder.

4. Pour the oil into the pan and cook the green beans for 6 minutes.

5. Put the pork mixture back to the pan.

6. Add the sauce and cook for 1 minute, stirring often.

Nutrients per Serving:

- Calories 312
- Fat 13.2 g
- Saturated fat 3.7 g
- Carbohydrates 18.6 g
- Fiber 5 g
- Protein 29.7 g
- Cholesterol 66 mg
- Sugars 8 g
- Sodium 634 mg
- Potassium 496 mg

Pork Pineapple Fried Rice

You're going to love this stir-fried rice with tender pork strips, ginger, carrots, pineapple, and celery. It's loaded with so much flavor and nutrients.

Serving Size: 4

Preparation Cooking Time: 45 minutes

Ingredients:

- 1 egg
- 2 egg whites
- 2 teaspoons vegetable oil
- 1 tablespoon vegetable oil
- 1 lb. pork tenderloin, sliced into strips
- 1 cup fresh pineapple chunks
- 1 stalk celery, sliced thinly
- 1 carrot, sliced thinly
- ½ cup scallions, chopped
- 2 cloves garlic, crushed and minced
- 2 teaspoons ginger, grated
- 2 cups cooked brown rice
- ½ cup peas
- 3 tablespoons low-sodium soy sauce
- 1 tablespoon fresh cilantro leaves, chopped

Instructions:

1. Beat the egg in a bowl.

2. Stir in the egg whites and beat to combine. Set aside.

3. Pour 2 teaspoons vegetable oil into a pan over medium high heat.

4. Stir fry the pork for 5 minutes.

5. Transfer to a plate.

6. Pour the remaining oil to the pan.

7. Cook the scallions, garlic, ginger, carrot, pineapple and celery for 4 minutes.

8. Add the eggs and cook for 10 seconds.

9. Stir in the cooked rice.

10. Cook while stirring for 1 minute.

11. Add the rest of the ingredients.

12. Cook while stirring for another 1 minute.

13. Serve immediately.

Nutrients per Serving:

- Calories 386
- Fat 10.7 g
- Saturated fat 1.8 g
- Carbohydrates 40.7 g
- Fiber 3.9 g
- Protein 30.9 g
- Cholesterol 144 mg
- Sugars 8 g
- Sodium 546 mg
- Potassium 585 mg

Pork Kimchi Stir Fry

Combining pork and Kimchi turns out to be a fantastic idea. Here's a quick and simple recipe that gives you a full delicious meal in 30 minutes.

Serving Size: 4

Preparation Cooking Time: 30 minutes

Ingredients:

- 1 teaspoon peanut oil
- 2 eggs, beaten
- 2 tablespoons vegetable oil
- 2 teaspoons garlic, crushed and minced
- 2 teaspoons ginger, grated
- 3 scallions, chopped
- 1 lb. pork tenderloin, trimmed and sliced into small pieces
- 1 cup carrots, diced
- 1 cup zucchini, diced
- 2 cups brown rice, cooked
- 3 tablespoons chili paste
- 1 cup Kimchi, chopped

Instructions:

1. Pour 1 teaspoon peanut oil into a pan over medium high heat.

2. Cook the eggs for 30 seconds.

3. Flip and cook for another 20 seconds.

4. Transfer the cooked eggs to a cutting board and slice.

5. Add the vegetable oil to the pan.

6. Stir fry the garlic, ginger and scallions for 30 seconds.

7. Add the pork and stir fry for 1 minute.

8. Stir in the carrots and zucchini.

9. Cook for 3 minutes.

10. Transfer to a plate.

11. Add the rice and cook while stirring for 2 minutes.

12. Put the pork, eggs and veggies back to the pan along with the chili paste and Kimchi.

13. Cook while stirring for 1 minute.

Nutrients per Serving:

- Calories 401
- Fat 14.5 g
- Saturated fat 3.3 g
- Carbohydrates 37.6 g
- Fiber 4.8 g
- Protein 29.3 g
- Cholesterol 153 mg
- Sugars 7 g
- Sodium 554 mg
- Potassium 679 mg

Pork with Zucchini Eggplant

This vibrant and colorful dish is also loaded with flavors that you'd love and nutrients you'd benefit from. It's a mix of pork strips, cherry tomatoes, zucchini, and eggplant.

Serving Size: 4

Preparation Cooking Time: 40 minutes

Ingredients:

Quinoa

- ¾ cup quinoa
- 1 ¼ cups water
- ½ cup fresh cilantro, chopped

Sauce

- 2 tablespoons white miso
- 3 tablespoons water
- 1 ½ tablespoons tahini (see Tips)
- 2 tablespoons rice vinegar
- 1 teaspoon ginger, grated
- 1 garlic, minced
- 1 tablespoon sesame oil

Veggies

- 3 tablespoons olive oil, divided
- 1 lb. lean ground pork
- 1 pint cherry tomatoes
- 1 zucchini, sliced into cubes
- 1 eggplant, sliced into cubes
- Salt to taste

Instructions:

1. Boil the quinoa and water in a pan.

2. Reduce heat and cover the pan.

3. Simmer for 15 minutes or until water is fully absorbed.

4. Remove from the stove.

5. Let sit for 5 minutes.

6. Add the cilantro.

7. Make the sauce by mixing the miso, water, tahini, vinegar, ginger, garlic and sesame oil in a bowl. Set aside.

8. Pour 1 tablespoon olive oil into a pan over medium heat.

9. Cook the pork for 6 minutes, stirring often.

10. Transfer the pork to a plate.

11. Pour in the remaining olive oil.

12. Stir fry the tomatoes, zucchini and eggplant for 7 minutes.

13. Put the pork back to the pan.

14. Add the quinoa to serving bowls.

15. Sprinkle the pork and vegetable mixture on top.

16. Drizzle with the reserved sauce.

Nutrients per Serving:

- Calories 452
- Fat 23 g
- Saturated fat 4.9 g
- Carbohydrates 33.3 g
- Fiber 5.8 g
- Protein 29.8 g
- Cholesterol 66 mg
- Sugars 7 g
- Sodium 673 mg
- Potassium 912 mg

Pork with Bok Choy Bell Pepper

Here's another quick and simple pork recipe that's also loaded with veggies for more flavor, texture, and nutrients. This stir-fry dish is drizzled with orange and lime sauce.

Serving Size: 4

Preparation Cooking Time: 30 minutes

Ingredients:

Sauce

- 1 tablespoon olive oil
- ¼ cup freshly squeezed orange juice
- ¼ cup freshly squeezed lime juice
- ¼ cup fresh cilantro, chopped
- 2 teaspoons cornstarch
- ½ teaspoon oregano
- ½ teaspoon cumin
- Salt and pepper to taste

Stir-Fry

- 3 tablespoons peanut oil, divided
- 1 lb. pork tenderloin, sliced into strips
- 1 cup scallions, chopped
- 3 cups red bell pepper, sliced into strips
- 4 cups bok choy, chopped
- 3 cloves garlic, crushed and minced

Instructions:

1. In a bowl, mix the olive oil, orange juice, lime juice, cilantro, cornstarch, oregano, cumin, salt and pepper.

2. Pour 1 tablespoon oil into the pan over high heat.

3. Stir fry the pork for 3 minutes.

4. Transfer to a plate.

5. Pour 1 tablespoon oil into the pan.

6. Stir fry the scallions and bell pepper for 2 minutes.

7. Add the remaining oil to the pan.

8. Stir fry the bok choy and garlic for 3 minutes.

9. Put the pork back to the pan along with the sauce.

10. Cook for 2 minutes, stirring often.

Nutrients per Serving:

- Calories 297
- Fat 17 g
- Saturated fat 3.2 g
- Carbohydrates 12.6 g
- Fiber 3 g
- Protein 23.9 g
- Cholesterol 60 mg
- Sugars 6 g
- Sodium 536 mg
- Potassium 796 mg

Sweet Sour Pork

Stir fry pork with tomato and pineapple and drizzle it with sweet, savory, and tangy sauce for a dinner meal that everyone will be satisfied with.

Serving Size: 4

Preparation Cooking Time: 45 minutes

Ingredients:

- 1 lb. boneless pork shoulder, fat trimmed and sliced into smaller pieces
- Salt and pepper to taste
- 1 tablespoon rice wine, divided
- 4 teaspoons low-sodium soy sauce, divided
- 1 tablespoon ginger, minced
- 3 ½ teaspoons cornstarch, divided
- 1 teaspoon toasted sesame oil
- 2 tablespoons vinegar
- 2 tablespoons pineapple juice
- 1 ½ teaspoons brown sugar
- 1 tablespoon ketchup
- 2 tablespoons peanut oil, divided
- ½ cup carrot, sliced
- 1 cup tomato, sliced thinly
- ¼ cup scallions, chopped
- 2 cups pineapple chunks

Instructions:

1. Season the pork with the salt, pepper, 2 teaspoons rice wine and half of the soy sauce.

2. Sprinkle with the minced ginger.

3. Coat with 2 teaspoons cornstarch.

4. Drizzle with the sesame oil.

5. In a bowl, mix the vinegar, pineapple juice, brown sugar and ketchup.

6. Stir in the remaining rice wine, remaining soy sauce, and remaining cornstarch.

7. Pour 1 tablespoon peanut oil into a pan over high heat.

8. Cook the pork for 2 minutes without stirring.

9. Stir fry for 1 minute.

10. Transfer to a plate.

11. Add the remaining oil to the pan.

12. Stir fry the carrot for 30 seconds.

13. Put the pork back to the pan.

14. Add the scallions and tomatoes.

15. Stir fry for 30 seconds.

16. Add the pineapple juice mixture with the pineapple chunks.

17. Stir fry for 2 minutes.

Nutrients per Serving:

- Calories 312
- Fat 16.8 g
- Saturated fat 4.6 g
- Carbohydrates 20.8 g
- Fiber 2.2 g
- Protein 18.7 g
- Cholesterol 65 mg
- Sugars 13 g
- Sodium 416 mg
- Potassium 462 mg

Pork Chop Suey

There's no need to leave the comforts of your own home and dine in a fancy Chinese restaurant to get a taste of this incredible dish.

Serving Size: 4

Preparation Cooking Time: 30 minutes

Ingredients:

- 3 tablespoons low-sodium soy sauce
- 1 cup low-sodium chicken stock
- Pepper to taste
- 2 tablespoons blackstrap molasses
- 5 teaspoons cornstarch
- 2 tablespoons vegetable oil, divided
- 1 lb. pork tenderloin, sliced into small pieces
- 1 onion, slivered
- 1 tablespoon ginger, minced
- 1 red bell pepper, sliced thinly
- 3 cups mung bean sprouts

Instructions:

1. Mix the soy sauce, broth, pepper and molasses in a bowl.

2. Take 2 tablespoons of this mixture and transfer to a smaller bowl.

3. Add the cornstarch to the smaller bowl. Stir and set aside.

4. Add the pork to the first mixture.

5. Cover and marinate for 15 minutes.

6. Pour 1 tablespoon vegetable oil into a pan over medium heat.

7. Stir fry the pork for 3 minutes.

8. Transfer to a bowl lined with paper towel.

9. Increase heat and add the remaining oil.

10. Stir fry the onion, ginger, bell pepper and bean sprouts for 3 minutes.

11. Add the broth mixture.

12. Bring to a boil.

13. Cook while stirring for 2 to 3 minutes.

14. Reduce heat. Pour in the reserved sauce.

15. Cook for 1 minute.

Nutrients per Serving:

- Calories 279
- Fat 9.8 g
- Saturated fat 1.4 g
- Carbohydrates 20.6 g
- Fiber 2.7 g
- Protein 28.2 g
- Cholesterol 74 mg
- Sugars 13 g
- Sodium 611 mg
- Potassium 942 mg

Pork with Napa Cabbage

An amazing fusion of flavors and textures—this is one dish that you'd certainly want to include more often in your menu at home.

Serving Size: 4

Preparation Cooking Time: 1 hour and 5 minutes

Ingredients:

- ¼ cup rice vinegar
- ¼ cup low-sodium soy sauce
- 1 clove garlic, chopped
- 2 tablespoons ginger, chopped and divided
- ½ teaspoon Chinese five-spice powder
- ¼ cup rice wine
- 3 teaspoons cornstarch, divided
- Pinch of sugar
- 1 lb. pork tenderloin, fat trimmed and sliced into strips
- 3 tablespoons peanut oil, divided
- ½ cup peanuts (unsalted)
- 6 cups napa cabbage, sliced into strips
- ½ cup scallions, chopped

Instructions:

1. Combine the rice vinegar, soy sauce, garlic, half of ginger, five-spice powder, rice wine, 1 teaspoon cornstarch and sugar in a bowl.

2. Coat the pork strips with the remaining cornstarch.

3. Pour 2 tablespoons peanut oil into a pan over high heat.

4. Cook the pork without stirring for 1 minute.

5. Stir fry for 3 minutes.

6. Transfer to a plate.

7. Add the remaining oil to the pan.

8. Add the remaining ginger along with the peanuts and cabbage.

9. Stir fry for 30 seconds.

10. Add the sauce and bring to a boil.

11. Put the pork back to the pan.

12. Reduce heat and simmer for 2 minutes.

13. Garnish with the scallions before serving.

Nutrients per Serving:

- Calories 384
- Fat 22.3 g
- Saturated fat 3 g
- Carbohydrates 12.5 g
- Fiber 4 g
- Protein 31.1 g
- Cholesterol 74 mg
- Sugars 1 g
- Sodium 608 mg
- Potassium 902 mg

Pork Spaghetti Squash Stir Fry

Most vegans make use of spaghetti squash to cook pasta. But this particular recipe is for meat lovers. It combines the delicious strands of this vegetable with flavorful and succulent pork strips.

Serving Size: 4

Preparation Cooking Time: 1 hour and 30 minutes

Ingredients:

- 3 lb. spaghetti squash
- 2 teaspoons toasted sesame oil
- 5 scallions, sliced thinly
- 1 tablespoon ginger, minced
- 2 cloves garlic, crushed and minced
- Salt to taste
- 1 lb. pork tenderloin, fat trimmed and sliced into strips
- 2 tablespoons low-sodium soy sauce
- 2 tablespoons rice vinegar
- 1 teaspoon chili sauce

Instructions:

1. Preheat your oven to 350 degrees F.

2. Slice the squash in half.

3. Scoop out the flesh and remove the seeds.

4. Bake the squash for 1 hour in the oven.

5. Let cool for 15 minutes before shredding the flesh into strands using a fork.

6. Pour the oil into a pan over medium high heat.

7. Cook the scallions, ginger and garlic.

8. Season with the salt.

9. Add the pork strips and stir fry for 3 minutes.

10. Stir in the squash and cook for 1 minute.

11. Stir in the rest of the ingredients and cook while stirring for 30 seconds.

Nutrients per Serving:

- Calories 224
- Fat 5.5 g
- Saturated fat 1.3 g
- Carbohydrates 18.6 g
- Fiber 4 g
- Protein 26.2 g
- Cholesterol 74 mg
- Sugars 7 g
- Sodium 679 mg
- Potassium 813 mg

Vegetables Fried Rice

If you want to minimize your consumption of meat, here's a fried rice recipe that you'd surely want to give a try.

Serving Size: 6

Preparation Cooking Time: 1 hour and 30 minutes

Ingredients:

- 8 oz. tofu, sliced into cubes
- 1 tablespoon hot sauce
- 6 teaspoons olive oil, divided
- ½ teaspoon fresh ginger, grated
- 2 carrots, sliced thinly
- 1 ½ cups edamame, shelled
- 1 cup snow pea pods
- 1 lb. asparagus spears, sliced
- 1 egg, beaten
- 2 teaspoons toasted sesame oil
- 2 cups long grain rice
- 8 oz. canned water chestnuts, rinsed, drained and sliced
- 2 tablespoons low-sodium soy sauce
- 1 tablespoon sesame seeds, toasted

Instructions:

1. Marinate the tofu cubes in hot sauce for 30 minutes.

2. Pour 2 teaspoons olive oil into a pan over medium heat.

3. Cook the ginger for 30 seconds.

4. Add the carrots and edamame and stir fry for 3 minutes.

5. Add the pea pods and asparagus.

6. Stir fry for 5 minutes.

7. Transfer the vegetables to a plate.

8. Pour 2 more teaspoons olive oil into the pan.

9. Cook the tofu for 5 minutes or until golden on all sides.

10. Add to the vegetable mixture.

11. Pour the remaining olive oil into the pan.

12. Add the egg and cook for 3 minutes.

13. Transfer to a cutting board, and slice into strips.

14. Transfer to a plate.

15. Pour the sesame oil to the pan.

16. Increase heat to medium high.

17. Place the cooked rice into the pan.

18. Add the tofu, veggies and eggs back to the pan.

19. Mix well.

20. Stir in the soy sauce and water chestnuts.

21. Cook for 2 minutes, stirring often.

22. Garnish with the sesame seeds and serve.

Nutrients per Serving:

- Calories 283
- Fat 11.5 g
- Saturated fat 1.7 g
- Carbohydrates 30 g
- Fiber 4.4 g
- Protein 15.3 g
- Cholesterol 19 mg
- Sugars 5 g
- Sodium 318 mg
- Potassium 225 mg

Snap Pea Asparagus Stir Fry

Dress up your veggies with Asian flavors for a simple but satisfying dinner meal.

Serving Size: 6

Preparation Cooking Time: 30 minutes

Ingredients:

- 1 tablespoon vegetable oil
- 2 cloves garlic, crushed and minced
- 2 teaspoons ginger, grated
- 1 onion, sliced thinly
- 1 red sweet pepper, sliced
- 1 lb. asparagus spears, trimmed and sliced
- 2 cups sugar snap peas
- 1 tablespoon sesame seeds
- 2 tablespoons low-sodium soy sauce
- 2 tablespoons rice vinegar
- 1 tablespoon brown sugar
- 1 teaspoon toasted sesame oil

Instructions:

1. Pour the vegetable oil into a pan over medium high heat.

2. Cook the garlic and ginger for 15 seconds.

3. Stir fry the onion, sweet pepper and asparagus for 3 minutes.

4. Add the sesame seeds and pea pods and cook while stirring for 3 minutes.

5. Add the rest of the ingredients.

6. Stir fry for 2 minutes.

Nutrients per Serving:

- Calories 86
- Fat 3.9 g
- Saturated fat 0.5 g
- Carbohydrates 10.2 g
- Fiber 3.1 g
- Protein 3.2 g
- Cholesterol 13 mg
- Sugars 6 g
- Sodium 188 mg
- Potassium 271 mg

Carrot Pea Pod Stir Fry

Stir fry carrot strips and pea pods in soy sauce, ginger, and garlic, and you get to have this simple but tasty dish that you can serve on the side of your main course.

Serving Size: 4

Preparation Cooking Time: 15 minutes

Ingredients:

- 2 teaspoons toasted sesame oil
- 2 cloves garlic, minced
- 2 teaspoons ginger, minced
- 1 cup carrot, sliced into thin strips
- 2 cups sugar snap pea pods
- 2 teaspoons low-sodium soy sauce

Instructions:

1. In a pan over medium high heat, add the oil and stir fry the garlic and ginger for 20 seconds.

2. Stir in the carrots and pea pods.

3. Cook for 5 minutes, stirring frequently.

4. Toss in soy sauce and serve.

Nutrients per Serving:

- Calories 50
- Fat 2.4 g
- Saturated fat 0.3 g
- Carbohydrates 6 g
- Fiber 1.6 g
- Protein 1.5 g
- Cholesterol 13 mg
- Sugars 3 g
- Sodium 109 mg
- Potassium 161 mg

Ginger Veggies Stir Fry

Once you get a taste of this aromatic stir fry dish, there's a good chance that you'd want to make this over and over. The simple dish combines water chestnuts, baby corn, and pea pods drizzled with ginger and soy sauce.

Serving Size: 6

Preparation Cooking Time: 30 minutes

Ingredients:

- 1 tablespoon low-sodium soy sauce
- ½ cup cold water
- ½ teaspoon ground ginger
- 1 teaspoon cornstarch
- 1 tablespoon vegetable oil
- 1 onion, chopped
- 1 clove garlic, crushed and minced
- 1 carrot, sliced thinly
- 2 cups cauliflower florets
- 8 oz. water chestnuts, drained and sliced
- 14 oz. baby corn, drained
- 1 red sweet pepper, sliced into strips
- ½ cup snap peas, trimmed

Instructions:

1. Mix the soy sauce, water, ginger and cornstarch in a bowl. Set aside.

2. In a pan over medium high heat, stir fry the onion, garlic, carrot and cauliflower for 7 minutes.

3. Add the water chestnuts, corn, sweet pepper and snap peas.

4. Stir fry for 2 to 3 minutes.

5. Pour in the soy sauce mixture.

6. Cook for 2 minutes or until the sauce has thickened.

Nutrients per Serving:

- Calories 56
- Fat 2 g
- Saturated fat 0 g
- Carbohydrates 7 g
- Fiber 2 g
- Protein 2 g
- Cholesterol 12 mg
- Sugars 3 g
- Sodium 77 mg
- Potassium 312 mg

Vegetable Curry

There's so much to love about this vegetable curry dish that's bursting with Asian flavors you'd definitely get addicted to.

Serving Size: 2

Preparation Cooking Time: 40 minutes

Ingredients:

- 1 teaspoon vegetable oil
- 1 onion, chopped
- ½ carrot, sliced
- Salt to taste
- 2 teaspoons freshly grated ginger
- 2 teaspoons curry paste
- 1 cup coconut milk (unsweetened)
- ½ cup chickpeas, rinsed and drained
- 1 cup green beans, trimmed and sliced
- ½ cup cauliflower florets
- 2 teaspoons freshly squeezed lime juice
- 1 cup brown rice, cooked
- 2 teaspoons peanuts, chopped
- 2 tablespoons cilantro leaves, chopped

Instructions:

1. Add the oil to a pan over medium heat.

2. Stir fry the onion and carrot for 6 minutes. Season with the salt.

3. Stir in the ginger and curry paste.

4. Cook for 1 minute, stirring frequently.

5. Pour in the coconut milk.

6. Bring to a boil.

7. Add the chickpeas, green beans and cauliflower.

8. Reduce heat and simmer for 7 to 8 minutes.

9. Add the lime juice.

10. Pour the veggie mixture on top of the rice.

11. Sprinkle the peanuts and cilantro on top.

Nutrients per Serving:

- Calories 259
- Fat 10.8 g
- Saturated fat 6.4 g
- Carbohydrates 34.9 g
- Fiber 6 g
- Protein 7.6 g
- Cholesterol 12 mg
- Sugars 7 g
- Sodium 535 mg
- Potassium 300 mg

Okra Stir Fry

Cooking okra in high heat eliminates the slimy texture that most people don't like. Seasoning okra with Indian chili powder, turmeric, and paprika gives you a tasty veggie stir fry that pairs well with brown rice.

Serving Size: 4

Preparation Cooking Time: 30 minutes

Ingredients:

- 2 tablespoons grapeseed oil
- ½ teaspoon cumin seeds
- ½ teaspoon mustard seeds
- 1 onion, sliced
- 5 cups okra, sliced
- Salt to taste
- 1 teaspoon paprika
- 2 teaspoons ground coriander
- 1 teaspoon Indian chili powder
- ½ teaspoon ground turmeric

Instructions:

1. Pour the oil into a pan over medium high heat.

2. Once hot, add the cumin seeds and mustard seeds.

3. Cook while stirring for 1 minute.

4. Reduce heat and add the onion.

5. Stir fry for 6 minutes.

6. Add the okra.

7. Increase heat to high.

8. Stir fry for 5 minutes.

9. Season with the salt, paprika, coriander, chili powder and turmeric.

10. Stir fry for another 5 minutes.

Nutrients per Serving:

- Calories 131
- Fat 7.5 g
- Saturated fat 0.6 g
- Carbohydrates 15.3 g
- Fiber 5.9 g
- Protein 3.5 g
- Cholesterol 12 mg
- Sugars 4 g
- Sodium 223 mg
- Potassium 504 mg

Bok Choy Stir Fry

Don't be fooled into thinking that this is a bland meal. Although it's not as vibrant and as colorful as other veggie stir-fries, this one doesn't disappoint you in terms of taste and texture, as it is cooked in a sauce that made with mustard and sherry vinegar.

Serving Size: 4

Preparation Cooking Time: 20 minutes

Ingredients:

- 1 teaspoon toasted sesame oil
- 1 teaspoon Dijon mustard
- 2 teaspoons sherry vinegar, divided
- 1 lb. baby bok choy, trimmed and sliced
- 2 tablespoons peanut oil
- 1 tablespoon garlic, crushed and minced
- Salt and pepper to taste
- 2 tablespoons dry sherry

Instructions:

1. Mix the sesame oil, mustard and half of the sherry vinegar in a bowl. Set aside.

2. Add peanut oil in a pan over high heat.

3. Stir fry the bok choy for 1 minute.

4. Season with the salt and pepper.

5. Drizzle with the vinegar.

6. Stir fry for 30 seconds.

7. Pour in the reserved sauce.

8. Remove from heat.

9. Toss to combine evenly.

Nutrients per Serving:

- Calories 92
- Fat 8.1 g
- Saturated fat 1.3 g
- Carbohydrates 2.9 g
- Fiber 1.2 g
- Protein 1.9 g
- Cholesterol 13 mg
- Sugars 1 g
- Sodium 346 mg
- Potassium 430 mg

Cabbage Carrots Stir Fry

For this recipe, it is recommended to use Chinese cabbage, also called Napa cabbage. Chinese cabbage is more tender and more flavorful than other types of cabbage.

Serving Size: 4

Preparation Cooking Time: 30 minutes

Ingredients:

Sauce

- 2 teaspoons oyster sauce
- 1 tablespoon dry sherry
- Salt to taste
- ¼ teaspoon sugar
- Cabbage and Carrots
- 2 tablespoons vegetable oil
- 2 teaspoons garlic, minced
- ¼ cup shallot, sliced thinly
- 1 carrot, sliced thinly
- 8 oz. Chinese cabbage, sliced thinly
- 1 teaspoon sesame oil

Instructions:

1. Mix the oyster sauce, sherry, salt and sugar in a bowl.

2. Pour the oil into a pan over high heat.

3. Stir fry the garlic and shallots for 10 seconds.

4. Add the carrot and cabbage.

5. Stir fry for 1 minute.

6. Pour the oyster sauce mixture into the pan.

7. Stir fry for another 1 minute.

8. Drizzle the sesame oil on top and serve.

Nutrients per Serving:

- Calories 114
- Fat 8.4 g
- Saturated fat 0.7 g
- Carbohydrates 8.1 g
- Fiber 2.3 g
- Protein 1.8 g
- Cholesterol 13 mg
- Sugars 3 g
- Sodium 231 mg
- Potassium 310 mg

Broccoli Tomato Stir Fry

You only need 20 minutes and a few ingredients to get this quick and simple stir-fry dish done.

Serving Size: 4

Preparation Cooking Time: 20 minutes

Ingredients:

Sauce

- 1 tablespoon rice wine
- Salt to taste
- ¼ teaspoon sugar
- 2 teaspoons oyster sauce
- Broccoli Tomatoes
- 1 tablespoon vegetable oil
- 1 tablespoon ginger, chopped
- 3 cups broccoli florets
- 1 cup cherry tomatoes, sliced in half
- 1 teaspoon sesame oil

Instructions:

1. Mix the rice wine, salt, sugar and oyster sauce in a bowl.

2. Pour the oil into a pan over high heat.

3. Once hot, stir fry the ginger for 10 to 15 seconds.

4. Add the broccoli and cook while stirring for 2 minutes.

5. Stir fry the tomatoes for 15 to 20 seconds.

6. Pour in the rice wine mixture.

7. Cover and simmer for 30 seconds.

8. Remove the cover and stir fry for 2 minutes.

9. Drizzle with the sesame oil.

Nutrients per Serving:

- Calories 74
- Fat 4.9 g
- Saturated fat 0.9 g
- Carbohydrates 5.8 g
- Fiber 2.2 g
- Protein 2.1 g
- Cholesterol 13 mg
- Sugars 2 g
- Sodium 218 mg
- Potassium 280 mg

Garden Stir Fry

This bright and cheery dish, which includes carrots, bell peppers, herbs, and spices, is made even more special with the addition of chicken-style seitan.

Serving Size: 4

Preparation Cooking Time: 35 minutes

Ingredients:

- ½ cup dry sherry
- 2 tablespoons freshly squeezed lime juice
- 2 tablespoons light brown sugar
- 2 tablespoons hoisin sauce
- Salt to taste
- 2 teaspoons cornstarch
- ½ cup water
- 2 tablespoons vegetable oil, divided
- 1 lb. chicken-style seitan, drained and sliced into smaller pieces
- 2 teaspoons ginger, minced
- ¼ cup peanuts, chopped
- 2 bell peppers, sliced thinly
- 4 carrots, sliced thinly
- ¼ cup cilantro, chopped

Instructions:

1. Combine the sherry, lime juice, brown sugar, hoisin sauce, salt, cornstarch and water in a bowl. Set aside.

2. Pour 1 tablespoon vegetable oil into a pan over medium high heat.

3. Cook the seitan for 5 minutes or until golden and crispy.

4. Add the remaining oil.

5. Stir fry the ginger and peanuts for 1 minute.

6. Add the bell peppers and carrots.

7. Stir fry for 1 minute.

8. Pour in the sauce.

9. Toss to coat evenly.

10. Reduce heat.

11. Cover the pan.

12. Cook for 4 minutes.

13. Stir in the fresh cilantro leaves before serving.

Nutrients per Serving:

- Calories 327
- Fat 12.1 g
- Saturated fat 1.3 g
- Carbohydrates 31.5 g
- Fiber 12.1 g
- Protein 20 g
- Cholesterol 13 mg
- Sugars 12 g
- Sodium 705 mg
- Potassium 434 mg

Tofu Mushroom Stir Fry

As you probably know, tofu and mushrooms are good together, as what this recipe proves once more.

Serving Size: 5

Preparation Cooking Time: 20 minutes

Ingredients:

- 4 tablespoons vegetable oil, divided
- 1 red bell pepper, diced
- 1 lb. mushrooms, sliced
- ½ cup scallions, trimmed and sliced
- 1 clove garlic, grated
- 1 tablespoon freshly grated ginger
- 8 oz. tofu, diced
- 3 tablespoons oyster sauce

Instructions:

1. Pour 2 tablespoons vegetable oil into a pan over high heat.

2. Stir fry the bell pepper and mushrooms for 4 minutes.

3. Add the scallions, garlic and ginger.

4. Cook while stirring for 30 seconds.

5. Transfer the vegetables to a plate.

6. Pour the remaining oil into the pan.

7. Cook the tofu for 4 minutes or until golden on all sides.

8. Add the oyster sauce and vegetables.

9. Stir fry for 1 minute.

Nutrients per Serving:

- Calories 171
- Fat 13.1 g
- Saturated fat 2.3 g
- Carbohydrates 8.6 g
- Fiber 2.3 g
- Protein 7.7 g
- Cholesterol 15 mg
- Sugars 3 g
- Sodium 309 mg
- Potassium 469 mg

Szechuan Tofu

Tofu is so versatile that you can flavor it up in various ways, season it with different herbs and spices, and pair it up with an array of veggies. In this recipe, we pair it up with green beans. But if these are not available in your kitchen, you can also use broccoli or carrots.

Serving Size: 4

Preparation Cooking Time: 30 minutes

Ingredients:

- ¼ cup low-sodium soy sauce
- ½ cup water, divided
- 2 teaspoons balsamic vinegar
- 1 tablespoon tomato paste
- ½ teaspoon red pepper flakes
- 1 teaspoon cornstarch
- 2 teaspoons sugar
- 14 oz. tofu, sliced into cubes
- 2 tablespoons cornstarch
- 2 tablespoons vegetable oil, divided
- 4 cloves garlic, crushed and minced
- 2 teaspoons ginger, minced
- 4 cups fresh green beans, trimmed and sliced in half

Instructions:

1. In a bowl, combine the soy sauce, ¼ cup water, balsamic vinegar, tomato paste, red pepper flakes, 1 teaspoon cornstarch and sugar. Set aside.

2. Coat the tofu cubes with the remaining cornstarch.

3. Pour 1 tablespoon vegetable oil into a pan over medium high heat.

4. Cook the tofu for 2 minutes without stirring.

5. Cook while stirring for 3 minutes.

6. Transfer to a plate lined with paper towels.

7. Reduce heat.

8. Pour the remaining oil into the pan.

9. Stir fry the garlic, ginger and green beans for 1 minute.

10. Add the soy sauce mixture.

11. Stir in the tofu.

12. Cook for 1 minute.

Nutrients per Serving:

- Calories 216
- Fat 11.5 g
- Saturated fat 1.5 g
- Carbohydrates 20.5 g
- Fiber 4.8 g
- Protein 11.8 g
- Cholesterol 15 mg
- Sugars 5 g
- Sodium 816 mg
- Potassium 352 mg

Korean Tofu

In this stir-fry recipe, we grill the tofu and serve it with stir-fried cabbage on the side. The barbecue sauce is made more enticing with the addition of chili paste.

Serving Size: 4

Preparation Cooking Time: 6 hours

Ingredients:

Tofu

- 3 tablespoons vegetable oil, divided
- 1 onion, chopped
- 2 tablespoons ginger, minced
- 2 tablespoons garlic, crushed and minced
- ¾ cup scallions, chopped
- ¼ cup low-sodium soy sauce
- 2 tablespoons Korean chili paste
- 2 tablespoons paprika
- 2 tablespoons rice vinegar
- 2 tablespoons water
- 1 tablespoon sesame oil
- 1 tablespoon honey
- 2 teaspoons white miso
- 2 teaspoons molasses
- 15 oz. tofu, sliced

Cabbage

- 2 tablespoons sesame oil
- 3 tablespoons low-sodium soy sauce
- 2 tablespoons peanut oil
- 1 cup scallions, chopped
- 12 cups Chinese cabbage, sliced thinly
- 2 tablespoon sesame seeds, divided

Instructions:

1. Prepare the glaze for the tofu by pouring 1 tablespoon vegetable oil into a pan over medium heat.

2. Add the onion and cook for 5 minutes.

3. Add the ginger and garlic.

4. Stir fry for 1 minute.

5. Remove from the stove.

6. Add the rest of the tofu ingredients to the pan except the tofu.

7. Mix well.

8. Transfer to a bowl.

9. Let cool for 15 minutes.

10. Spread the tofu cubes in a baking pan.

11. Coat evenly with the sauce.

12. Cover with foil.

13. Refrigerate for 4 hours.

14. When ready to cook, preheat the grill.

15. Brush the tofu with the remaining vegetable oil.

16. Grill for 5 minutes per side.

17. Transfer to a plate.

18. Prepare the cabbage by pouring the sesame oil and soy sauce in a bowl.

19. Add the peanut oil to a pan over high heat.

20. Once hot, add the scallions and cook for 3 minutes, stirring.

21. Add the cabbage and stir fry for 3 minutes.

22. Pour in the sesame oil mixture and the sesame seeds.

23. Serve the tofu with the cabbage stir fry.

Nutrients per Serving:

- Calories 389
- Fat 31 g
- Saturated fat 5 g
- Carbohydrates 18.5 g
- Fiber 7.2 g
- Protein 16.3 g
- Cholesterol 19 mg
- Sugars 5 g
- Sodium 759 mg
- Potassium 871 mg

Tofu with Cashews Peas

Tofu drenched in hoisin sauce and stir fried with cashews and peas create a satisfying and flavorful meal to serve during dinner time with the family.

Serving Size: 4

Preparation Cooking Time: 50 minutes

Ingredients:

- ½ teaspoon chili-garlic sauce
- 3 tablespoons hoisin sauce
- 2 tablespoons low-sodium soy sauce
- 2 tablespoons vegetable oil, divided
- 14 oz. tofu, sliced into cubes
- 2 cloves garlic, crushed and minced
- 1 cup onion, chopped
- 1 tablespoon ginger, grated
- 8 oz. sugar snap peas, trimmed
- 8 oz. snow peas, trimmed
- 1 cup peas
- ½ cup cashews, sliced in half

Instructions:

1. In a bowl, combine the chili garlic sauce, hoisin sauce and soy sauce.

2. Pour 1 tablespoon oil into a pan over medium high heat.

3. Add the tofu and cook for 8 minutes.

4. Transfer the tofu to a plate lined with paper towels.

5. Add the remaining oil into the pan.

6. Stir fry the garlic, onion and ginger for 1 minute.

7. Add the three types of peas and stir fry for 3 minutes.

8. Add the tofu back to the pan.

9. Pour in the sauce and stir in the cashews.

10. Cook while stirring for 1 minute.

Nutrients per Serving:

- Calories 353
- Fat 19.7 g
- Saturated fat 3.1 g
- Carbohydrates 30.9 g
- Fiber 7.1 g
- Protein 16.6 g
- Cholesterol 16 mg
- Sugars 12 g
- Sodium 567 mg
- Potassium 483 mg

Maple Barbecue Tofu

Here's a different way of making barbecue sauce—make it using maple syrup. This is what makes this tofu stir-fry extra special.

Serving Size: 4

Preparation Cooking Time: 1 hour and 20 minutes

Ingredients:

- Barbecue sauce
- 2 teaspoons vegetable oil
- 1 onion, chopped
- 5 cloves garlic, crushed and minced
- ½ cup apple juice
- ¾ cup cider vinegar
- 1 tablespoon Worcestershire sauce
- ¾ cup low-sodium ketchup
- 1 tablespoon Dijon mustard
- ¼ cup maple syrup
- 1 ½ teaspoons hot sauce
- Tofu with Vegetables
- 14 oz. tofu, sliced into cubes
- 4 teaspoons vegetable oil, divided
- 3 oz. mushrooms, sliced
- 1 cup cauliflower florets
- 2 carrots, grated
- 1 cup broccoli florets

Instructions:

1. Pour the oil into a pan over medium heat.

2. Add the onion and cook for 5 minutes.

3. Stir in the garlic and the rest of the sauce ingredients.

4. Bring to a simmer.

5. Reduce heat and cook for 30 minutes.

6. Let cool and then transfer to a blender.

7. Puree until smooth.

8. Pour 2 tablespoons oil into a pan over medium high heat.

9. Cook the tofu for 6 minutes.

10. Pour in the remaining vegetable oil.

11. Add the mushrooms, cauliflower, carrots and broccoli.

12. Stir fry for 4 minutes.

13. Pour the sauce.

14. Add the tofu.

15. Cook for 3 minutes and then serve.

Nutrients per Serving:

- Calories 227
- Fat 10.1 g
- Saturated fat 1.4 g
- Carbohydrates 20.5 g
- Fiber 3.3 g
- Protein 10.6 g
- Cholesterol 17 mg
- Sugars 13 g
- Sodium 108 mg
- Potassium 576 mg

Shrimp Fried Rice

There's no need for elaborate preps when you make use of stir-fry recipes such as this one--shrimp and egg tossed in fried rice and seasoned with herbs and spices.

Serving Size: 4

Preparation Cooking Time: 40 minutes

Ingredients:

- 2 tablespoons vegetable oil
- 1 tablespoon ginger, minced
- 1 tablespoon garlic, minced
- ¼ teaspoon red pepper flakes
- 1 cup carrots, diced
- 1 cup mushrooms, sliced
- 4 oz. shrimp, peeled and deveined
- 2 cups sugar snap peas, trimmed and sliced in half
- 2 eggs, beaten
- 2 tablespoons low-sodium soy sauce
- Pepper to taste
- 4 cups cooked rice, refrigerated overnight

Instructions:

1. Pour the oil into a pan over high heat.

2. Stir fry the ginger, garlic and red pepper flakes for 10 seconds.

3. Add the mushrooms and carrots.

4. Cook while stirring for 1 minute.

5. Stir in the shrimp and cook for 1 minute.

6. Add the snap peas and stir fry for another minute.

7. Stir in the rest of the ingredients.

8. Cook until the eggs are set.

9. Serve warm.

Nutrients per Serving:

- Calories 301
- Fat 9.9 g
- Saturated fat 1.9 g
- Carbohydrates 38.3 g
- Fiber 3.5 g
- Protein 14.2 g
- Cholesterol 138 mg
- Sugars 5 g
- Sodium 512 mg
- Potassium 514 mg

Shrimp in Hoisin Sauce

Red pepper flakes add a little zing to this flavorful dish that centers on orange shrimp drenched in hoisin sauce.

Serving Size: 2

Preparation Cooking Time: 40 minutes

Ingredients:

- 1 tablespoon cooking oil, divided
- 6 oz. shrimp, peeled and deveined
- 1 clove garlic, crushed and minced
- 1 red sweet pepper, sliced into thin strips
- 4 teaspoons hoisin sauce
- 3 tablespoons freshly squeezed orange juice
- 1 cup spinach, shredded
- 1 cup cooked rice
- Red pepper flakes

Instructions:

1. Pour ½ tablespoon oil into a pan over medium high heat.

2. Cook the garlic for 15 seconds.

3. Add the sweet pepper and stir fry for 3 minutes.

4. Transfer to a plate.

5. Pour the remaining oil into the pan.

6. Stir fry the shrimp for 3 minutes.

7. Pour in the hoisin sauce and orange juice.

8. Bring to a boil.

9. Reduce heat and simmer for 1 minute.

10. Put the garlic, sweet pepper and shrimp back to the pan.

11. Stir in the spinach.

12. Serve with cooked rice sprinkled with red pepper flakes on top.

Nutrients per Serving:

- Calories 300
- Fat 9.4 g
- Saturated fat 1.5 g
- Carbohydrates 32.6 g
- Fiber 1.4 g
- Protein 20.7 g
- Cholesterol 129 mg
- Sugars 6 g
- Sodium 269 mg
- Potassium 337 mg

Salt Pepper Shrimp

This dish is a popular option in many Chinese restaurants. Make your own with less sodium and fat by using this healthy recipe.

Serving Size: 2

Preparation Cooking Time: 30 minutes

Ingredients:

- 2 tablespoons freshly squeezed lime juice
- 1 tablespoon vegetable oil
- ½ teaspoon sugar
- 2 teaspoons low-sodium soy sauce
- 1 red bell pepper, sliced thinly
- 3 cups Chinese cabbage
- Salt and pepper to taste
- 2 teaspoons toasted sesame oil
- 2 tablespoons rice flour
- 10 oz. shrimp, peeled and deveined
- 1 serrano pepper, minced
- ½ teaspoon five-spice powder

Instructions:

1. Combine the sesame oil, lime juice, sugar, and soy sauce in a bowl.

2. Stir in the bell pepper and cabbage.

3. In another bowl, mix the salt, pepper, five spice powder and rice flour.

4. Coat the shrimp with this mixture.

5. Pour the oil into a pan over medium high heat.

6. Cook the shrimp for 3 minutes, stirring often.

7. Add the Serrano pepper and stir fry for 1 minute.

8. Serve with the cabbage slaw.

Nutrients per Serving:

- Calories 296
- Fat 13.6 g
- Saturated fat 1.6 g
- Carbohydrates 20.1 g
- Fiber 2.9 g
- Protein 23.5 g
- Cholesterol 191 mg
- Sugars 5 g
- Sodium 1191 mg
- Potassium 309 mg

Shrimp with Mango Spicy Basil

Here's a shrimp stir fry recipe that would make you feel like you're in the tropics with every bite. The shrimp are tossed in mangoes and spicy basil. For sure, you won't get enough of this.

Serving Size: 4

Preparation Cooking Time: 45 minutes

Ingredients:

    1 lb. shrimp, peeled and deveined

    Salt to taste

    Pinch cayenne pepper

    ¼ teaspoon ground turmeric

    1 tablespoon olive oil

    ¼ cup basil leaves, chopped

    ½ cup scallions, sliced thinly

    1 mango, sliced into cubes

Instructions:

1. Season the shrimp with the turmeric, cayenne and salt.

2. Wrap in foil.

3. Refrigerate for 30 minutes.

4. Pour the oil into a pan over medium heat.

5. Cook the shrimp for 1 minute.

6. Flip and cook for another 1 minute.

7. Add the rest of the ingredients and stir fry for 1 minute.

Nutrients per Serving:

Calories 158

Fat 5 g

Saturated fat 0.9 g

Carbohydrates 12.2 g

Fiber 1.7 g

Protein 16.5 g

Cholesterol 143 mg

Sugars 9 g

Sodium 792 mg

Potassium 307 mg

Shrimp with Eggplant Green Beans

This incredibly simple but delicious shrimp stir-fry recipe comes with eggplant and green beans tossed in chili sauce with ginger and lemon.

Serving Size: 4

Preparation Cooking Time: 30 minutes

Ingredients:

Sauce

- 2 tablespoons freshly squeezed lemon juice
- ¼ cup Korean chili paste
- 1 tablespoon soy sauce
- 1 tablespoon ginger, grated
- 2 teaspoons sugar
- 1 tablespoon sesame oil
- 1 tablespoon dry sherry

Stir-Fry

- 3 tablespoons peanut oil, divided
- 1 lb. shrimp, peeled and deveined
- 3 cups eggplant, sliced
- ¼ cup scallions, trimmed and sliced
- 3 cloves garlic, crushed and minced
- 4 cups green beans, trimmed and sliced in half

Instructions:

1. Prepare the sauce by mixing all the sauce ingredients in a bowl.

2. Pour 1 tablespoon peanut oil into a pan over medium heat.

3. Stir fry the shrimp for 3 minutes.

4. Transfer the shrimp into a plate.

5. Add 1 tablespoon oil to the pan.

6. Stir fry the scallions and eggplant for 2 minutes.

7. Pour the remaining oil and stir fry the green beans and garlic for 3 minutes.

8. Put the shrimp back to the pan.

9. Stir in the sauce and cook for 2 more minutes.

Nutrients per Serving:

    Calories 277

    Fat 14.6 g

    Saturated fat 2.4 g

    Carbohydrates 16.9 g

    Fiber 5.2 g

    Protein 22.8 g

    Cholesterol 159 mg

    Sugars 5 g

    Sodium 561 mg

    Potassium 650 mg

Conclusion

As you can see, stir fries can be your go-to dishes whenever you think you don't have enough time to prepare meals in the kitchen.

Even though some of the recipes require a lot of dicing and slicing, remember that these steps can be made ahead of time so that when it's time for you to cook, it will take you only a few minutes to get the dish done.

Not to mention, stir fries are also considered healthy, as long as you use organic and natural ingredients, and you don't load up on too much oil and salt.

If you are going to make use of sauces and seasonings, opt for those that are lower in sodium. If you are going to use beef or pork, choose lean cuts that won't shoot up your cholesterol levels.

So are you ready to give these recipes a try?

Don't waste a second more and get started!

About the Author

A native of Albuquerque, New Mexico, Sophia Freeman found her calling in the culinary arts when she enrolled at the Sante Fe School of Cooking. Freeman decided to take a year after graduation and travel around Europe, sampling the cuisine from small bistros and family owned restaurants from Italy to Portugal. Her bubbly personality and inquisitive nature made her popular with the locals in the villages and when she finished her trip and came home, she had made friends for life in the places she had visited. She also came home with a deeper understanding of European cuisine.

Freeman went to work at one of Albuquerque's 5-star restaurants as a sous-chef and soon worked her way up to head chef. The restaurant began to feature Freeman's original dishes as specials on the menu and soon after, she began to write e-books with her recipes. Sophia's dishes mix local flavours with European inspiration making them irresistible to the diners in her restaurant and the online community.

Freeman's experience in Europe didn't just teach her new ways of cooking, but also unique methods of presentation. Using rich sauces, crisp vegetables and meat cooked to perfection, she creates a stunning display as well as a delectable dish. She has won many local awards for her cuisine and she continues to delight her diners with her culinary masterpieces.

* * * ★ ★ ★ ★ ★ ★ ★ * * *

Author's Afterthoughts

I want to convey my big thanks to all of my readers who have taken the time to read my book. Readers like you make my work so rewarding and I cherish each and every one of you.

Grateful cannot describe how I feel when I know that someone has chosen my work over all of the choices available online. I hope you enjoyed the book as much as I enjoyed writing it.

Feedback from my readers is how I grow and learn as a chef and an author. Please take the time to let me know your thoughts by leaving a review on Amazon so I and your fellow readers can learn from your experience.

My deepest thanks,

Sophia Freeman

Subscribe to the Newsletter!

https://sophia.subscribemenow.com/

* * * ★ ★ ★ ★ ★ ★ ★ * * *

Printed in Great Britain
by Amazon